HAGAR, UNLOVED & UNWANTED

NIYI BORIRE - PAUL ONUKAOGU
- SENAYON AMOSU - HERVE KADIYA -
OMOR BELLO - RUTH EJIWALE
- TOFUNMI EJIWALE

Hagar, Unloved & Unwanted

© Changemakers International Book Club 2021

All rights reserved.

No part of this publication may be reproduced, distributed, or transmitted in any form or by any means, including photocopying, recording, or any other electronic or mechanical method, without the prior written permission of the author, except in the case of brief quotations embodied in critical reviews and certain other non-commercial uses permitted by copyright law.

All scriptural quotations are taken from the New Living Translation (NLT)

Dedication

To everyone who has felt unloved, lost, or insignificant, this book is dedicated to you.

This is a reminder that God sees you and you are never alone.

Though you may feel abandoned and used, remember that there is hope, and just like He did for Hagar, He is making a way in the midst of it all.

'Then Jesus said, *"Come to me, all of you who are weary and carry heavy burdens, and I will give you rest'*. Matthew 11:28 (NLT)

Acknowledgements

Special thanks to the people who worked so hard in the preparation and the completion of this book.

We appreciate our families for their support, love, and encouragement.

And also, thanks to everyone who spared time out of their busy schedule to attend meetings in order to participate in this work. Your effort is much appreciated and will not go in vain.

Table of Content

Dedication	v
Acknowledgements	vi
Table of Content	vii
Introduction	viii
Chapter 1 - Hagar - Background	1
Chapter 2 - Hagar and Abraham	15
Chapter 3 - Hagar and Sarah	51
Chapter 4 - Hagar and Ishmael	75
Chapter 5 - Hagar and God	87
Chapter 6 - Hagar and You	101
Meet the Authors	115

Introduction

To be unloved and unwanted is not something that many people can handle, especially in our world today. This explains why depression, suicidal thoughts, and suicide are on the rise like never before. People all over the world are facing rejection in one form or the other and at one level or another. It's a demon we all face. Sometimes, we defeat it; other times, it floors us. Everyone has a deep-seated desire to be loved and wanted, but that is not always the case.

In this book, we take you, the reader, on a memorable and meaningful journey into Hagar's life in her present time. We also journey through her story whilst drawing lessons and touching on a vast array of subjects from surrogacy to abandonment to hearing from God and other topics that greatly affected women then and strongly affect many women today.

This is in no way a book for women alone, even though the main character is a woman. Instead, Hagar is only an example through which we examine significant life challenges and draw inspiration and gain practical wisdom that would help us get better results in our own lives today.

This woman knew what it was to feel unloved, want revenge, suffer disappointment, and feel unwanted, yet also found the courage to go forward in life. She is the woman who cried out to God. For a long time, she defined herself by her past because she saw no future to long for until God interrupted her and gave her something to look forward to.

Are you a wandering soul that has felt unloved or unwanted? Your 'well' is waiting for you in the pages of this book. Just take a leap of faith and go along on this journey with Hagar.

HAGAR – BACKGROUND

Hagar's first mention in the Bible was in the first five verses of Genesis Chapter 16.

"Now Sarai, Abram's wife, had not been able to bear children for him. But she had an Egyptian servant named Hagar. So Sarai said to Abram, "The LORD has prevented me from having children. Go and sleep with my servant. Perhaps I can have children through her." And Abram agreed with Sarai's proposal. So Sarai, Abram's wife, took Hagar the Egyptian servant and gave her to Abram as a wife. (This happened ten years after Abram had settled in the land of Canaan.) So Abram had sexual relations with Hagar, and

she became pregnant. But when Hagar knew she was pregnant, she began to treat her mistress, Sarai, with contempt. Then Sarai said to Abram, "This is all your fault! I put my servant into your arms, but now that she's pregnant she treats me with contempt. The LORD will show who's wrong—you or me!" Abram replied, "Look, she is your servant, so deal with her as you see fit." Then Sarai treated Hagar so harshly that she finally ran away'. Genesis 16:1-5 (NLT)

From her introduction in the scriptures, we know a few things upfront about her; she was a slave and an Egyptian, called 'Hagar'. Hagar's name has no particular meaning. Hagar was probably in her early teens when she was taken to be Sarah's slave from Egypt. After Abraham and Sarah had stayed ten years in Canaan, Sarah gave Hagar to Abraham to take her as his wife, and her only reason for doing this was to have children through Hagar. Isn't that interesting? We would see the implications and consequences of that as we go on. Abraham, without any form of hesitance, went in to Hagar, and she got pregnant. Mission accomplished!

After Hagar got pregnant, The Bible says that she began to despise her mistress, Sarah, seeing that she now had what her mistress badly wanted – a child. Sarah, who initiated the plan to start with, could not withstand one of the by-products of her choice. She resorted to maltreating Hagar and eventually asked that she be sent away. While fleeing from the maltreatment of her mistress, Hagar met an angel.

Both the Qur'an and the Torah are unified that Hagar was an Egyptian princess who was given as a slave to Sarah and Abraham. Some accounts say Hagar was the daughter of Pharaoh and was given to Abraham and Sarah because of the good fortune they brought to Egypt while they stayed there.

We have no idea of her background, but we know that ancient Egyptians sold themselves and their children into bonded labour – not willingly but because they could not pay off their debts.

In those days, most slaves were owned by men. So, Hagar was not a general slave. Hagar was explicitly assigned to Sarah by Abraham to care for her needs. Even though Abraham later took Hagar as a wife, they never stopped seeing her as a slave. That was her identity before them, and nothing was going to change that, not even bearing the first child of her master. Hagar must have felt very insignificant because the Bible constantly recognised her as a slave. She didn't have an identity; all she was known as was Sarah's slave. She must have had an identity crisis.

The most likely narrative is that Hagar was from a poor background. That was probably how she ended up in slavery because it is doubtful that Pharaoh will let his daughter become a slave to a man who is a non-Egyptian. The Egyptian civilization was the most sophisticated civilization at the time. The Egyptians would have thought that they were of a higher social class than any other nation.

Hagar was born into a low-income family. She probably struggled growing up like every other person, figuring out her place in society and why she was disadvantaged. It is also very likely that Hagar became a slave very early as most kids do. Most girls were already working in slavery even before puberty. There are places in the world, even today, where 8-year-olds have to look after babies. They have to grow up very quickly to take charge of adult duties.

Hagar would have had to grow up very quickly. She would have had to learn to survive and be independent. She would have had to learn how to get things done in the home, take care of house chores, and be a woman very early. She would have been very diligent; otherwise, she wouldn't have been a prized asset to start with.

Abraham was a rich man and would have been a multimillionaire in today's world (Genesis 13:2). You can't become the handmaid of the wife of a man like Richard Branson without being hardworking and intelligent. She would have had to be excellent at what she does to be Sarah's personal assistant. She would have had to be on top of things. From her childhood, she must have been trained to work hard to thrive in Sarah's courtyard despite being relatively young.

Hagar must also have been a beautiful young woman for Sarah to recommend that she bear a child with her husband. Most surrogates today are always pretty and decent, and there was no way Sarah would have given an unattractive slave to Abraham to carry his seed, no matter how talented she was.

The whole story teaches us that even talented and blessed people like Abraham and Sarah have their fair share of tough times. Being rich or wealthy doesn't preclude anyone from facing the uncertainties of life. Challenges don't respect status. While it may be easier for the wealthy to handle certain life challenges because of their status and substance, they are not exempted from the pain and stress that come with life's challenges.

Hagar was Sarah's handmaid. A handmaid is a 'personal servant'. It has to be someone you can trust because that person can kill you. Handmaids know everything about your personal life that other people can't see. For Sarah to choose Hagar as her handmaid, she must have been intelligent, organised, and pretty. Hagar was blessed, but she was a slave, much like Joseph in Potiphar's house. He was a slave, but he was young, talented, consistently applied himself, and hardworking. He was young, but he managed everything in Potiphar's house.

People can have lots of gifts and endowments and still be in situations that they cannot control. A lot of events in Hagar's life were beyond her control – she couldn't control where she lived; she couldn't control her freedom, she couldn't control her choice of a husband; she couldn't control the conception of her son, but there she is with a lot of gifts that God had blessed her with even though she was an imperfect woman.

How can you be so blessed yet limited? How can you be full of potentials that you lack the freedom to control? Don't we all seek to be in control of our lives, even though it could hurt God's plans for our lives sometimes? We all secretly desire to be in charge of our lives, dictating our movements, deciding our choices, and revelling in our abilities. Hagar definitely wasn't left out in this.

Beyond Your Limitations, You Are Valuable

Ten years after she lived with Sarah and Abraham, she moved from being just a slave to becoming a wife. It happened just like that. She wasn't given the opportunity to decide here. For ten years of obscurity, nothing was said about her in the Bible. The Biblical introduction of Hagar came ten years after she was sold into slavery. Her introduction happened when there was a need. Hagar was a solution to the problem of that household. Does that sound familiar?

You, reading this right now, are carrying the solutions to the problems of this world and may not know. When Hagar arrived at the household of Abraham, she didn't look like the solution that she was. But after ten years, she had gone through puberty and emotional development. She had more confidence and had grown in those ten years.

Even if Hagar was a solution, she wasn't ready in Egypt. It took a process, and it is the same for many of us who carry solutions that will benefit other people. Right now, we find ourselves in very uncomfortable circumstances like Joseph and Hagar. However, we should never think we are incapable of offering value when we are in difficult situations in life. Hagar offered value even though she was in a difficult situation. She was blessed enough to be chosen to be the mother of the firstborn son of Abraham.

It took a process of ten years of development for Hagar to get to the point of offering value to the household of Abraham. You need to realise that oftentimes, the processes that get us ready for the time when the value we carry will be needed are not palatable. To get well-refined gold from a bar of scrap gold, the scrap gold must be subjected to fire for long hours, and the process itself could be very tedious. What fire does for gold is to help it attain its highest value level. This is the same way the seemingly unpleasant experiences (abuse, maltreatment, etc.) we go through help bring us to that point where our value is highest and most needed.

> *'The king of Aram had great admiration for Naaman, the commander of his army, because through him the LORD had given Aram great victories. But though Naaman was a mighty warrior, he suffered from leprosy. At this time Aramean raiders had invaded the land of Israel, and among their captives was a young girl who had been given to Naaman's wife as a maid. One day the girl said to her mistress, "I wish my master would go to see the prophet in Samaria. He would heal him of his leprosy. So Naaman told the king what the young girl from Israel had said'.* 2 Kings 5:1-4 (NLT)

The story above speaks of another little slave who was of value. The little maid actually helped Naaman get cured of his leprosy. She ordinarily did not qualify as someone to be heard, not to talk of being listened to. Slaves were generally treated as minors and were hardly seen as solution providers. However, in this scenario, the little maid had superior knowledge that could help save her master. Because she had a solution, she was listened to.

It's straightforward to assume that you are your limitation. It's very easy to measure your worth by the nature of your struggles. But you need to understand that you are more valuable than your situation, no matter how demeaning, belittling, or disheartening it is.

Even though Hagar was just a slave, she was still valuable. She may not have meant so much to her master and his wife, but she meant so much to God. At least, that was proven by the intervention of an angel when she was left all alone with her son to die in the wilderness. God showed up to save her. That was a communication of her worth by God.

It didn't matter that she had been used and dumped. It didn't matter that her consent was not sought. It didn't matter that she was just a slave whose destiny could be toyed with by the desire of another woman. She was still valuable to God.

When it mattered the most, she had something to offer more than being a slave. She had something to offer more than doing chores and running errands. At least, she had something that her master's wife didn't have.

This should serve as an encouragement for you. Life may have relegated you to the position of a slave where you have little or no say. **The circumstances of life may have put you in a place where you doubt that any good thing can come out of you. You must remember that you are not your limitations.** God knows you by name. God knows who you are. God is mindful of you. God has made you valuable. Yes, you have something to offer. Don't look down on yourself. Don't define yourself by your limitations. You are more valuable than you think you are.

Contemplation

1. What about your background or upbringing don't you like or feel has disadvantaged you in life?

2. If you could change anything in your past, what would it be?

3. Is there any challenge or limitation you were faced with or are faced with presently that has affected your sense of self-worth?

Chapter 2

HAGAR AND ABRAHAM

'Now Sarai, Abram's wife, had not been able to bear children for him. But she had an Egyptian servant named Hagar. So Sarai said to Abram, "The LORD has prevented me from having children. Go and sleep with my servant. Perhaps I can have children through her." And Abram agreed with Sarai's proposal. So Sarai, Abram's wife, took Hagar the Egyptian servant and gave her to Abram as a wife. (This happened ten years after Abram had settled in the land of Canaan.) So Abram had sexual relations with Hagar, and she became pregnant. But when Hagar knew she was pregnant, she began to treat her mistress, Sarai, with contempt'. Genesis 16:1-4 (NLT)

Abraham was a man from a good background who God told to leave his father's house to a land where He would show him. He took that step of faith in obedience. Apparently, at the time, his marriage was already under a lot of stress because they didn't have a child, and Abraham was 75 years old when God asked him to leave his father's house.

When Abraham got to Canaan, he discovered a famine in the land God had led him to. This is a lesson for many people that there are many times when God gives a divine instruction to take a step, and when you get there, you find out it is not like what you planned. Many people get into businesses, relationships, careers, projects with the backing of God and explicit instruction but still find it challenging to execute.

Abraham got there and was frustrated because he had brought a big family with him. So, he went to Egypt. During his sojourn in Egypt, he acquired a lot of wealth and had a lot of servants and slaves, one of which was probably Hagar.

A few years later, Abraham came back to Bethel, and while he was there, he built an altar, reconnected with his God, and started with his life in the land that God had called him to.

> *"After Lot had gone, the Lord said to Abram, "Look as far as you can see in every direction—north and south, east and west. I am giving all this land, as far as you can see, to you and your descendants[a] as a permanent possession. And I will give you so many descendants that, like the dust of the earth, they cannot be counted!"* Genesis 13:14-16 (NLT)

He still had a problem despite having so much wealth and was prosperous in gold, silver, and cattle. He still didn't have a child, and he was now about 85 years old. At this time, it was pretty frustrating for him because after he had returned from Egypt, Lot, his nephew, separated from him and took the best part of the land. At that time, Lot had a seed, and Abraham didn't. Maybe that was why Abraham allowed his nephew to take the best part of the land.

That same day after Lot left, God appeared to Abraham and made him a promise that his seed would be more than the stars of the sky. At the time of this promise, Abraham was almost ninety years old, and his wife was already postmenopausal.

Abraham had a promise of not just being prosperous but having a vast progeny, yet his reality didn't align because he was still childless and had just been betrayed by his nephew. Here he was stressed, anxious, and with a wife who was unhappy that she could not conceive. Imagine how life was in the house of Abraham. They had all the money, but they had no child. God had made a promise to Abraham about his seed, yet he did not have the one thing he desired the most.

Abraham was very vulnerable. There are people who are very comfortable in many areas of their life, but they are never happy. What that leads to is seeking an alternative, and Hagar was Abraham's alternative. **Hagar was never the first choice. Abraham didn't love Hagar. She was an alternative.**

We know Abraham was probably as tired as Sarah from the Bible, but he didn't do anything about their childlessness because he was the stronger person in their relationship. He had faith in God until Sarah brought the option of him marrying Hagar. It must be noted that Abraham actually took Hagar to be his wife. The Hebrew word *'nashiym'* (translated as 'wife'), which was used to describe Sarah, was also used to refer to Hagar in Gen. 16:3.

There are a lot of questions surrounding why Abraham agreed to marry Hagar. It could be he was very tired and accepted anything to please his wife. At his age, he probably would have made peace with his predicament and had assumed that he might never have children considering his wife was already postmenopausal at the time. Abraham took his nephew, Lot, with him on the journey to Canaan to probably serve as his heir. The promise from God invigorated his anxieties and put him under a lot of pressure. Abraham was also under pressure from Sarah, his wife. That would have affected his decision-making.

The Imbalance In the Marriage between Abraham And Hagar

'So Sarai said to Abram, "The LORD has prevented me from having children. Go and sleep with my servant. Perhaps I can have children through her." And Abram agreed with Sarai's proposal. So Sarai, Abram's wife, took Hagar the Egyptian servant and gave her to Abram as a wife. (This happened ten years after Abram had settled in the land of Canaan.) Genesis 16:2-3 (NLT)

Intent Imbalance

The idea of the marriage from the beginning was to give Sarah a child. Hagar's consent was not sought, so Hagar was merely seen as an object to satisfy a need. There was no consideration for her emotions in the picture. It was about fulfilling the promise of an offspring. The family that Hagar was going to be making was technically Sarah's family. Imagine Hagar becoming a wife in an unusual relationship without her volition. The purpose of the marriage was to benefit Abraham and Sarah. Hagar's interest was not considered.

Age Imbalance

There was a massive imbalance in the ages of Abraham and Hagar. They had different life experiences since Abraham was old enough to be her grandfather. They were generations apart which would definitely have affected how they saw and processed things, their preferences, etc. But all of that didn't matter because Hagar had no chance to make a choice.

It was customary for a mistress to give their slave to their husband to bear children for them in their day and time. This also happened in Jacob's time.

Dream/Vision Imbalance

Another imbalance is that Abraham had a promise, Hagar did not. Abraham received a word from God for himself and his wife, which influenced the kind of dream about the future that they had, but Hagar was not a part of it.

Sometimes, we run with other people's dreams and visions. It doesn't have to benefit you, and there are a lot of people who do that today.

Sometimes, people sacrifice their dream for other people's dreams. That is not a bad thing, but you ought to find your purpose in all of that. The question is - what was Hagar's purpose?

Hagar's marriage to Abraham did not invalidate her servitude to Sarah. Regardless of her marriage to Abraham, she was still a slave. Hagar was only a wife in the room; she just had the title. She didn't get any love and affection from Abraham. There was no emotional commitment in the marriage.

Faith, Patience, and the Promise

Abraham and Sarah were impatient, they succumbed to the pressure of their childlessness despite their age, and they dragged Hagar into all of it. This marriage was a result of impatience, and it was not the perfect will of God. Abraham and Sarah got to a breaking point and tried to help God fulfil the promise, and in doing that, they changed the life of a young woman forever. It turned out for good because Ishmael lives on today through his progeny, but Hagar went through the pain. This was essentially a marriage of convenience.

This is quite relatable as it is what many of us do consciously or unconsciously many times. We receive God's promise about a situation in our lives, and we begin to seek ways in which we can make it happen at our time and pace. We simply try to achieve by the flesh what God has designed by the Spirit. The result is predictable – we end up messing up God's plan for our lives.

> *'Then you will not become spiritually dull and indifferent. Instead, you will follow the example of those who are going to inherit God's promises because of their faith and endurance'.* Hebrews 6:12 (NLT)

The scripture above is very instructive. It explains the requirements for inheriting or obtaining the promises of God for our lives.

Faith and endurance (patience) are the primary requirements for obtaining or stepping into God's promises for our lives. It is apparent that one cannot work without the other. So let's look at both more closely.

Faith, according to the Bible, *Faith shows the reality of what we hope for; it is the evidence of things we cannot see.* (Hebrews 11:1 NLT). This shows that faith is not something physical but can affect something physical. What does that mean? Hebrews 11:3 (NLT) sheds some light, *'By faith we understand that the entire universe was formed at God's command, that what we now see did not come from anything that can be seen'*. God was the first demonstrator of faith in the Bible. At creation, He commanded things into existence so that what we now see around us was not made from what can be seen.

Faith, which is unseen, has the power to bring into reality the things that can be seen. And as we have seen from the scriptures above, faith works by the Word of God. Faith is implanted or activated by God's Word. So, when God assured

Abraham that he was going to father his child, what that word was meant to do was to build faith in Abraham. It was designed to help him believe. Because without faith, it is impossible to please God or even receive anything from Him (Hebrews 11:6).

As you read this, can you cast your mind back to the numerous promises of God to you over the years? Many times, what God has promised looks very distant and impossible, judging by other physical parameters around us. This was precisely where Abraham and Sarah found themselves. What they could see around them didn't look like what God said they would see. So, they desperately sought to fill that gap like most of us would do. They figured that they could help God. The only help we can offer to God in actualising His promise to us is to believe what He has said and cooperate with the process that would bring it about.

Faith, however, doesn't work in isolation. It requires patience. You need the patience to follow through with the process that would deliver the promise to you. Patience refers to tolerance or forbearance. It is the ability to not only stay through the process but to stay faithful in the process. Walking in faith is working in faith. Faith is not passive; it is an active thing. Faith is work!

Look at this scripture again,

> *'Then you will not become spiritually dull and indifferent. Instead, you will follow the example of those who are going to inherit God's promises because of their faith and endurance''*. Hebrews 6:12 (NLT)

The promise is not for indifferent or slothful people. It means you cannot afford to be lazy when it comes to believing God based on His Word. Trying to help God by doing something we feel is right (and not what is right based on His instruction to and expectation of us) is being slothful. One would think that being slothful here means not doing something at all (like a state of inactiveness).

Being slothful here refers to engaging in the wrong action. This is corroborated by the story of the talent in Matthew 25. The master had given three of his servants' talents according to their ability. The ones who received five and two multiplied what they were given, but the servant who received one talent hid it. This was the master's response to him,

> *'But the master replied, 'You wicked and lazy servant! If you knew I harvested crops I didn't plant and gathered crops I didn't cultivate, why didn't you deposit my money in the bank? At least I could have gotten some interest on it.' "Then he ordered, 'Take the money from this servant, and give it to the one with the ten bags of silver. To those who use well what they are given, even more will be given, and they will have an abundance. But from those who do nothing, even what little they have will be taken away'.* Matthew 25:26-29 (NLT)

It's incredible to know that the servant with one talent was referred to as *'wicked and lazy'* for hiding the talent he was given instead of saving it, at least. The problem wasn't his inaction but wrong action. He at least hid the talent in the ground. That's some work, isn't it?

Abraham and Sarah acted by turning Hagar into a baby-making object. That's some energy expended, but it was in the wrong direction. It wasn't a God-inspired or God-instructed action; instead, it was a self-inspired and self-proclaimed action. And every time we try to put ourselves above the will and authority of God, it always ends in trouble. We must always allow God to bring His promises to pass in our lives.

There are a whole lot of things involved that are way beyond our human understanding. Hence, we will always need faith and patience, faith to take God by His Word, and patience to hold on to that word until it materialises. To further drive this point home, let's look at two examples (from the Bible) of people who obtained the promise through faith and patience.

Joseph, the Prime Minister

We have talked about him previously. However, it's good to dig a little deeper into his life to pick a few lessons that could help us better understand what we need to do to see God's promises come to pass in our lives; the importance of faith and patience. Let's see how Joseph was introduced in the Bible;

'This is the account of Jacob and his family. When Joseph was seventeen years old, he often tended his father's flocks. He worked for his half brothers, the sons of his father's wives Bilhah and Zilpah. But Joseph reported to his father some of the bad things his brothers were doing. Jacob loved Joseph more than any of his other children because Joseph had been born to him in his old age. So one day, Jacob had a special gift made for Joseph—a beautiful robe. But his brothers hated Joseph because their father loved him more than the rest of them. They couldn't say a kind word to him. One night Joseph had a dream, and when he told his brothers about it, they hated him more

than ever. "Listen to this dream," he said. "We were out in the field, tying up bundles of grain. Suddenly my bundle stood up, and your bundles all gathered around and bowed low before mine!" His brothers responded, "So you think you will be our king, do you? Do you actually think you will reign over us?" And they hated him all the more because of his dreams and the way he talked about them. Soon Joseph had another dream, and again he told his brothers about it. "Listen, I have had another dream," he said. "The sun, moon, and eleven stars bowed low before me!" This time he told the dream to his father as well as to his brothers, but his father scolded him. "What kind of dream is that?" he asked. "Will your mother and I and your brothers actually come and bow to the ground before you?" But while his brothers were jealous of Joseph, his father wondered what the dreams meant'. Genesis 37:2-11 (NLT)

Joseph is introduced to us, for the first time, as an outspoken teenager, loved by his father, hated by his brothers, and had a dream of a glorious future (which made his brothers even hate him more). Interestingly, he had two different dreams that pointed at the same thing – he was going to be a leader that even his family would bow to. Unlike Abraham, who heard God speak to him about His promise (that he would become a father of many generations), Joseph didn't hear God audibly; he just had a dream. The promise of God for his life came as a dream that could not leave his heart.

This is perhaps where many of us are today. We may not be able to identify with Abraham as it has to do with the promise of God to him, but we can relate to Joseph's dreams because we have dreams about a glorious future that have stayed with us for long. Like Joseph, our dreams are so graphic and easy to interpret by anyone who cares to listen. For us, that is God's unmistakable promise. It assures us of a good ending.

What could be more exciting and reassuring for a teenager as the certainty of being a leader that others will look up to and also worship? Joseph must have pictured how that dream would become a reality, and he most likely thought it would be so soon, perhaps by the time he was 20 years old. Don't we all assume that the beautiful picture of the future God has put in our hearts will become a reality in the shortest possible time?

Joseph could never have preempted the series of activities that would precede his eventual emergence as the leader he was ordained to be. The beautiful picture of the future he had seen kicked off as a nightmare. The first shocker for him was that he was sold into slavery by his brothers who hated him, firstly because their father loved him more and secondly because he had a dream that suggested that Joseph was going to be greater than them. He was even fortunate that they didn't kill him, which was the initial plan. (Genesis 37:12-36)

The same Joseph, who had seen himself as someone that others will bow to and serve, found himself in the position of a slave in Potiphar's house in Egypt. However, he took it in good spirit and gave his best to serving in his master's house so much that he distinguished himself. In no time, Potiphar noticed his exemplary leadership qualities even as a slave but much more; he noticed that the hand of God was upon Joseph, and he appointed him as the overseer over his house. Of course, that meant increased responsibility, but Joseph was up to the task.

In the line of duty, an opportunity came for Joseph to help God. His master's wife developed an interest in him as the young, industrious, and handsome young man that he was. Potiphar's wife made sexual advances at Joseph, which he resisted. What if he considered it as an opportunity to overthrow his master and become powerful in Egypt? What if he saw it as an opportunity to use his master's wife to do his bidding and work his way to the top? This is what many young people will consider today but not Joseph. He refused to compromise his integrity. And that landed him in prison eventually after his master's wife framed him up for attempted rape.

Here was Joseph, in prison for a crime he didn't commit. How bad could things get in the way of obtaining the promise of God for our lives? In the physical, things were certainly not looking bright for the young Joseph. But somehow, he still kept his faith. How do we know? Joseph got the chance to be a blessing to two of Pharaoh's officials who were in prison with him (the Butler and Baker). Unfortunately, they both dreamt and had trouble understanding what it meant.

The Butler's dream was the favourable one, and he was the best person to help Joseph get to the palace by way of recommendation. So, Joseph tried to explore that option,

> 'Within three days, Pharaoh will lift you up and restore you to your position as his chief cup-bearer. And please remember me and do me a favor when things go well for you. Mention me to Pharaoh, so he might let me out of this place. For I was kidnapped from my homeland, the land of the Hebrews, and now I'm here in prison, but I did nothing to deserve it'. Genesis 40:13-15 (NLT)

Joseph still believed that he could live a better life. He still thought that there was something out there worth living for. He still believed that he was created for more, hence the need to be recommended to Pharaoh. He probably concluded that, at last, his opportunity to fulfil his dream was finally here. But he still needed to wait two whole years more in prison. The butler completely forgot about Joseph after he was reinstated into Pharaoh's service. That must have been frustrating for Joseph.

Are there not times in our lives when we are so sure that certain people are in the best positions to help us expedite the actualisation of our dreams or God's promise to us? This could be the result of the access, connection, or possessions of these people. It's often a thin line between still trusting in God and relying on the arm of flesh, though. So while God uses men to help fulfil His promises for our lives, we must understand that we still need to trust God to do it the way only He can.

After two full years, Joseph's time of being showcased and elevated finally came (Genesis 41). Pharaoh had a dream that was so disturbing, and no one could interpret it in the entire kingdom. It was at this point that the Butler finally remembered Joseph. The time when the value he carried was needed showed up eventually. He did interpret Pharaoh's dream and recommended a solution that qualified him as the only man worthy of executing it. This was how Joseph became the prime minister of Egypt, and his dream came to pass precisely how he had seen it while he was 17 years old.

It's interesting to know that Joseph began to see the picture of the future God had ordained for him while he was 17 years old, but he had to wait for 13 years before it became a reality (as he became the prime minister of Egypt when he was 30 years old). For 13 years, Joseph had to wait patiently while keeping the faith to obtain God's promise. It's not enough to receive or know God's promise for your life; you must be willing to stay through the process that would make it a reality.

David, the King

David was introduced to us as the shepherd boy who was almost forgotten by his father when he was asked by the prophet Samuel to present his sons before God. See the account here,

> *'Now the LORD said to Samuel, "You have mourned long enough for Saul. I have rejected him as king of Israel, so fill your flask with olive oil and go to Bethlehem. Find a man named Jesse who lives there, for I have selected one of his sons to be my king." But Samuel asked, "How can I do that? If Saul hears about it, he will kill me." "Take a heifer with you," the LORD replied, "and say that you have come to make a sacrifice to the LORD. Invite Jesse to the sacrifice, and I will show you which of his sons to anoint for me." So Samuel did as the LORD instructed. When he arrived at Bethlehem, the elders of the town came trembling to meet him. "What's wrong?" they asked. "Do you come in peace?" "Yes," Samuel replied. "I have come to sacrifice to the LORD. Purify*

yourselves and come with me to the sacrifice." Then Samuel performed the purification rite for Jesse and his sons and invited them to the sacrifice, too. When they arrived, Samuel took one look at Eliab and thought, "Surely this is the LORD's anointed!" But the LORD said to Samuel, "Don't judge by his appearance or height, for I have rejected him. The LORD doesn't see things the way you see them. People judge by outward appearance, but the LORD looks at the heart." Then Jesse told his son Abinadab to step forward and walk in front of Samuel. But Samuel said, "This is not the one the LORD has chosen." Next Jesse summoned Shimea. but Samuel said, "Neither is this the one the LORD has chosen." In the same way all seven of Jesse's sons were presented to Samuel. But Samuel said to Jesse, "The LORD has not chosen any of these." Then Samuel asked, "Are these all the sons you have?" "There is still the youngest," Jesse replied. "But he's out in the fields watching the sheep and goats." "Send for him at once,"

Samuel said. "We will not sit down to eat until he arrives." So Jesse sent for him. He was dark and handsome, with beautiful eyes. And the LORD said, "This is the one; anoint him." So as David stood there among his brothers, Samuel took the flask of olive oil he had brought and anointed David with the oil. And the Spirit of the LORD came powerfully upon David from that day on. Then Samuel returned to Ramah'. 1 Samuel 16:1-13 (NLT)

David was the last born of eight brothers, but David seemed out of favour, unlike Joseph, who was his father's favourite. Or what explanation can be given to the fact that a father paraded his sons before the prophet and completely forgot that there was one left who was away in the field tending the sheep? So David appeared to have been overlooked by his family when it mattered the most. And that must have felt quite painful. This is an experience many of us can relate to because we have been there at one time or the other.

David's story is interesting because God chose him to be the next king of Israel while Saul was still on the throne. Saul had been rejected as king because of his disobedience and disregard for God's instruction. God's replacement for Saul was David. David had no clue what was coming; it wasn't his ambition, neither was it a matter of qualification; it was purely God's grace of election at work.

There are times when God decides to favour a man. Such was the case with David. God singled him out for honour as king, and he was anointed as king while the reigning king was still on the throne. It is believed that David was between 15-17 years old when he was anointed as the king of Israel. One would have thought that David would have promptly ascended the throne by divine orchestration, but that was not the case. A lot of things happened afterwards. David got enlisted into King Saul's service, killed the greatest enemy of Israel – Goliath, became a threat to the king and was turned into a fugitive as a result. The same king almost killed him he was to take over from.

Why would God elect David as king, get him anointed, yet he still had to run for his life? Couldn't God have made it so easy for David to ascend the throne after he was anointed? These are questions that may have crossed David's mind or anyone who reads his story today. We all often assume that God's involvement in our lives, especially when it is a promise, should make things very easy without any form of opposition.

After all, it wasn't David that chose to be king. He was busy doing his thing when he was sent for to be anointed as king. Why should his life then become tough just because God chose him? It took David another 13 to 15 years before he ascended the throne as king. Who would have thought it was going to take that long? Perhaps there were times when he doubted the anointing (which was a symbol of God's election and proof that it was a done deal). He probably felt that God had changed His mind. It didn't look like he would get there eventually, but he did.

David had the opportunity to kill Saul twice, which would have been a fast track to the throne (1 Samuel 24:1-22; 26:1-26). Yet, he would not seek a shortcut by hurting God's anointed. Though he had justifiable reasons to kill Saul, he chose the right way, not the easy way. In fact, his men were convinced that God presented David the opportunity, and they encouraged him to seize the opportunity. However, David had other ideas. He understood God's Word. He still saw Saul as God's anointed even though we all know that God had already rejected him as king many years before these incidences.

We all need discernment and openness of mind to understand that it is not all opportunities that come our way to help God fulfil His promise or plan for our lives that we must take. We must maintain our composure and not mess things up as Abraham and Sarah did. David waited patiently while keeping the faith until God worked things out the way only He could.

Process Gets You Ready for the Promise

We have looked at two examples from the Bible to highlight the importance of faith and patience in obtaining God's promise. As we close this section, it is crucial to underscore that obtaining God's promise through faith and patience is a process.

According to WordWeb Pro, a process is a sustained phenomenon or one marked by gradual changes through a series of states. This definition further shows that, just like we saw in the lives of Joseph and David, God often takes us through the 'process' journey to finetune us for what He has prepared for us.

The process we go through before laying hold of God's promise is not always palatable, as we saw in both examples above. However, the hardships, delays, trials, disappointments, struggles, etc., that we encounter while we wait for the manifestation of God's word all work together to build the right attitude and character to step into, enjoy, and keep what God has promised.

'And we know that God causes everything to work together for the good of those who love God and are called according to his purpose for them'. Romans 8:28 (NLT).

God knows how to make everything work together (even the seemingly unpleasant things) to favour His plans and purposes for our lives. Learn to see your waiting time as your making time. God doesn't bless us with what we cannot handle. So, if need be, He would rather delay the time of our possession until He is confident we have developed the strength of character to handle the promise.

How the Marriage between Hagar and Abraham Ended

'The LORD kept his word and did for Sarah exactly what he had promised. She became pregnant, and she gave birth to a son for Abraham in his old age. This happened at just the time God had said it would. And Abraham named their son Isaac. When Isaac grew up and was about to be weaned, Abraham

prepared a huge feast to celebrate the occasion. But Sarah saw Ishmael—the son of Abraham and her Egyptian servant Hagar—making fun of her son, Isaac. So she turned to Abraham and demanded, "Get rid of that slave woman and her son. He is not going to share the inheritance with my son, Isaac. I won't have it!" This upset Abraham very much because Ishmael was his son. But God told Abraham, "Do not be upset over the boy and your servant. Do whatever Sarah tells you, for Isaac is the son through whom your descendants will be counted. But I will also make a nation of the descendants of Hagar's son because he is your son, too." So Abraham got up early the next morning, prepared food and a container of water, and strapped them on Hagar's shoulders. Then he sent her away with their son, and she wandered aimlessly in the wilderness of Beersheba'. Genesis 21:1-3, 8-14 (NLT)

God honoured His Word to Abraham. Even though he and his wife tried to help God achieve the promise of a son, He still came through for them at His appointed time. Sarah eventually gave birth to a son just as He had promised. This automatically meant that Hagar was no longer as important as they initially thought she was in their lives.

The moment Isaac showed up on the scene and was mocked by his brother, Ishmael, trouble loomed for Hagar. Suddenly, she was no longer needed – and Ishmael too. Sarah wasn't willing to have Ishmael as an heir contender with Isaac. Didn't she think about that before giving Hagar to Abraham as a wife? Was she not expecting to give birth to her son as God had promised?

This looks more like creating a problem for yourself and then crying about it afterwards. The whole marriage thing between Abraham and Hagar was Sarah's idea to start with. It was a selfish move because it was all about Sarah. The only thing on her mind was getting a child. She didn't weigh the consequences well. And this is what happens in our lives many times, too, when we make a short-sighted decision. You shouldn't make a decision that has a long-term effect on a short-sighted basis. It would be best if you counted the cost well.

Desperation is not a good decision-maker. Life decisions should be made from the place of deep introspection and prayer. The consequences of our actions should be well considered before going ahead. Perhaps, Sarah would have had a rethink if she knew the gravity of her action when she insisted that Hagar should become their surrogate.

When it dawned on Sarah that Ishmael was going to be a problem for Isaac, she thought about how she could undo what she started, and she came up with another selfish idea – sending Hagar and her son away. She immediately communicated her desire to her husband and expected strict compliance just like the first time. Sarah appeared to have been a controlling kind of person.

Abraham couldn't argue with his wife upon her request even though it was a painful move for him. So he had to send Hagar and their son away. This was a traumatic end to a marriage that was one-sided to start with. They never even had a conversation. This was a marriage that was concocted and terminated without Hagar's volition. The same people (Abraham and Sarah) who got her into the marriage also sent her away without her consent. That would have been unfair and painful.

In the first place, a marital union should begin on a consensual basis which was not the case between Abraham and Hagar. Also, the dissolution of such a relationship should involve both parties. However, Hagar was not given a chance here. Her emotional investment in the marriage was certainly not considered. To cut her off like that without communication and consideration for her emotions was quite unfair.

Every kind of divorce has consequences that are not always palatable. However, it's usually more devastating when one party's opinion or emotion is not considered like it was in Hagar's case.

Contemplation

1. What about your background or upbringing don't you like or feel has disadvantaged you in life?

2. If you could change anything in your past, what would it be?

3. Is there any challenge or limitation you were faced with or are faced with presently that has affected your sense of self-worth?

HAGAR AND SARAH

Hagar was an Egyptian slave who served directly under Sarah. She was at a disadvantage from the get-go among the Hebrew women since she was a foreigner. That's ironic because she came from a nation that was more socially and politically advanced than Canaan.

The Dynamics between Hagar and Sarah

Sarah decided to give Hagar to Abraham to sleep with. The practice of giving another woman to your husband to sleep with, back then, wasn't strange. Hagar was not consulted in the matter, but Hagar could have jumped at the opportunity of sleeping with her master since that would have been a ticket to freedom.

Hagar became pregnant, and everything about the relationship between Sarah and Hagar shifted. Sarah was obviously not happy about the pregnancy. She felt as though Hagar had lost respect for her, and it devastated her. Imagine someone who was in a lower social class than you suddenly gain some leverage over you. So it wasn't crazy for Sarah to act the way she did. If Hagar was helping matters by showing compassion to Sarah, the story would have been different.

Hagar was one of Sarah's closest servants, and since the whole idea of sleeping with Abraham was Sarah's idea, not Hagar's, we can say that there was a form of trust between Sarah and Hagar. No one brings someone they don't trust to be a surrogate mother for their child.

Sarah was Abraham's wife who couldn't have a child, and age was not on her side, so the pressure was mounting because her husband, Abraham, received a prophecy from God that his descendants shall be as numerous as the stars in the sky. Sarah would have been very anxious about the fulfilment of the promise. She probably was scared that Abraham would marry another woman. Sarah was under a lot of pressure. With all things working well, no woman would bring a maid for her husband to sleep with.

Many times when God gives us a vision, we often try to interpret or work it out. God will give us a vision of a future or a destination, and He may not tell us how to get there. God gave Abraham a vision of the future that his progeny would be as many as the stars of the sky. God had seen the future, the ending even before the beginning, and He did not tell them how they would get there. They turned to Hagar as their way to their future, but Hagar was not God's instruction. Hagar was just a distraction.

A distraction is an attraction that vies for our attention. Distractions are always attractive. Hagar was not in their plan, but somehow, they got Hagar involved. Sometimes when God gives us a vision, He does not break it down into the process it would take to come to pass. As we saw earlier, God only told Joseph he would be a leader; He did not tell Joseph the journey he would go through. There is a progressive revelation of God's will. God gives us the revelation in bits, and even when God tells you the end, He may not tell you all the different processes you will go through to get there.

God gave Abraham this magnificent vision, and he made a mistake we often make as humans of trying to deliver that mandate. We feel pressure to help God by getting involved in the way everything will be fulfilled. But, most of the time, what God wants from us is our yielding. So we run the risk of wanting to help.

Looking at Sarah, you see a woman who wanted a child badly, and the intensity of her desire for a child was also fuelled by her husband, who had a dream of raising a nation from his loins. God had even changed their names from Abram (which means *"exalted father"*) to Abraham (which means *"father of many nations"*) and Sarai (which means *"princess"*) to Sarah (which means my princess and also denotes that she will be a mother of many nations). Sarah was blessed with many things, but she didn't have what she wanted the most – a child.

As humans, we may be blessed with many things, but we usually let what we don't have blind us from what we have. That underlies the reason why Hagar came into the picture for Sarah and her husband. The story would have been very different if they were grateful for what they had and patient enough to hang on to their faith for a few more years. They were only being humans because many of us wouldn't have done any better if we were in their shoes at the time. If there had been less pressure on Sarah, she wouldn't have gone the route that she went. Instead, she was internally and externally stressed by a revelation from God, which put her in a place of vulnerability that made her feel she needed to make an alternative since she couldn't bear any children.

Sarah made a choice, and she was the first recorded woman in the Bible who raised a child via a surrogate. However, she didn't believe that she could give birth to children because she laughed when the prophecy came that she would bear children (Genesis 18:12).

The Relationship between Hagar and Sarah before She Slept with Abraham

Hagar revered Sarah because she was the slave and Sarah was her mistress. So Hagar was probably worshipping Sarah, and their relationship was a *Slave-Mistress* kind of relationship.

Hagar was probably a special maid, and there was a level of trust between them. There are domestic servants in our world today who have that level of trust with their bosses, and they are almost like members of the family they work for. Sarah must have had a sense of dependability on Hagar that she could carry out any task perfectly.

Before you call somebody to be your surrogate, that person must be good-looking and hard working. Sarah would not elevate Hagar to that position without a level of trust. Hagar was probably Sarah's favourite servant.

Another point of view would be that Sarah chose Hagar as a surrogate because she wanted someone she could control because of her desperation; if not, she should have selected another Hebrew woman. To consider someone for surrogacy, Sarah would have considered her slaves one after the other, and Hagar definitely emerged as the best candidate after whatever criteria of scrutiny she used.

Therefore, the relationship between Hagar and Sarah before she slept with Abraham, and picked up the duties of a wife like her mistress, was a reverential kind of relationship from Hagar's end. She revered her mistress as is required of a slave in her mistress' house. And Sarah related to Hagar as a mistress will relate to her maid. The boundaries were clear. No familiarity whatsoever. It was strictly a formal kind of relationship.

The Relationship between Hagar and Sarah after Hagar Slept with Abraham

After Hagar slept with Abraham, the Bible says that she began to disrespect Sarah, her mistress. Again, this would likely be as a result of the familiarity with Abraham. After that encounter, Hagar saw Abraham differently, which affected her attitude towards Sarah as well. That gives credence to the famous proverb, *'Familiarity breeds contempt'*, which simply means loss of respect for someone (who was once held in high esteem) because of a closer association with the person.

After Hagar got pregnant, she felt she now had some form of leverage and that the position for the woman of the house was open for a contest with Sarah. This was because she now had what Sarah had not been able to give Abraham as she got pregnant very fast and easily. Sarah, who wanted someone she could control, as usual, could no longer get what she wanted since Hagar started acting up.

That tells a lot about us, humans when we are exposed to power or some form of leverage in our lives. There was a switch in the mentality of Hagar towards Sarah, which triggered Sarah's unfair treatment towards Hagar.

> *'So Abram had sexual relations with Hagar, and she became pregnant. But when Hagar knew she was pregnant, she began to treat her mistress, Sarai, with contempt. Then Sarai said to Abram, "This is all your fault! I put my servant into your arms, but now that she's pregnant she treats me with contempt. The LORD will show who's wrong—you or me!" Abram replied, "Look, she is your servant, so deal with her as you see fit." Then Sarai treated Hagar so harshly that she finally ran away'.* Genesis 16:4-6 (NLT)

Sarah blamed Abraham for Hagar's attitude towards her. However, Abraham allowed Sarah to handle the situation because getting Hagar pregnant wasn't his idea; it was Sarah's. So he let her handle it.

There is a risk for your ego to become inflated after you have achieved something significant. Hagar knew she had something they wanted. When she knew she was about to give that couple their heart's desire, she began to treat Sarah with contempt. So many times, we get in the way of God using us because of what we have achieved. Hagar wasn't grounded or level-headed enough to handle the situation.

That contact or familiarity Hagar had with Abraham brought about her shift in attitude. Familiarity breeds contempt. You can't blame Hagar because this was her opportunity not to die as a slave. She was probably beginning to imagine life as another mistress to her mistress' husband. That would certainly turn things around for her, and it definitely felt like a good possibility. We will handle a lot of conflicting situations better if only we can handle our emotions properly.

Abraham should have handled things better. Abraham should have found a way to discuss the situation with Hagar because she was carrying their child. Abraham should have called her to order, but Abraham absolved himself of every responsibility, giving Sarah the chance to act harshly towards Hagar to the point that she was sent away. Abraham could have prevented all of that from happening.

In life, you are not always going to get what you want. So when you are in difficult situations, analyse the problem first before reacting. Think of the consequences of your actions before you carry them out, don't act, and start blaming other people. You must always take responsibility for your actions and face the consequences. So let's consider a little more closely how to analyse situations before acting.

Situation Analysis

Daily, we all find ourselves in varying situations that require us to take action. And many times, our actions or inactions in response to those situations directly or indirectly affect other people. It is, therefore, imperative that we learn how to analyse situations well before taking action. If we look back, we often realise that certain decisions we made in the past could have yielded better results if we had analysed the situation better.

The first thing to note is that decisions should never be made based on feelings alone. This is because, many times, our emotions are not reliable; they can be very fleeting. Decisions need to be made rationally and not irrationally. However, we are not always on the rational side of things because of many factors.

There are a few things to consider when analysing a situation that would ensure that better decisions are made. Below are a few of them:

1. **Find out your role in it:** Whether directly or in complicity, we play a role in the situations we find ourselves in per time. So, the first thing to do in effectively analysing a situation is to find out our role in it. How did we contribute to it? What did we do or not do that put us in that situation? This requires objectivity.

2. **Admit your part in it:** After finding out the role you played in arriving at that situation, you must admit it. Own up to your contribution to it. Don't try to feign ignorance. Take responsibility for it.

3. **What is the best course of action:** Now that you have found yourself in that situation, what is the best thing to do, and how should it be done? How are you meant to approach the situation to ensure the best outcome possible?

4. **Who are the people also affected:** Every situation we find ourselves in, per time, often affects other people too, whether equally or to some degree. So it's important to consider other people involved and to what extent.

5. **How will your action affect others:** You need to consider how your action(s) in that situation will affect others concerned, and it should guide you to act in their best interests.

6. **Weigh the consequences:** Every action or inaction has consequences. Therefore, it is

important that you count the cost of your actions or inactions as far as the situation is concerned. Would you be proud of the result? Would it make your life and that of others better? Would it inspire faith and hope in those who will hear about it later? Would it glorify God and portray you as His representative?

These elements considered above would always help us to better analyse situations before acting. They will ensure that we do things that we can be proud of even many years later. If Sarah, Abraham, and Hagar had weighed the matter well, they could have acted better individually. It has been many years after their actions, but the consequences are still with us today. The descendants of Ishmael are still a pain in the neck of the descendants of Isaac. Trying to help God may have immediate personal benefits, but it also has long-term generational implications. Hence, the need to think well before acting.

Relationship Evolution

Life happens. Sometimes, relationships can be altered by circumstances. For Hagar, life happened. She was in that household at the moment they needed a child; she was called upon, and she stepped up. Based on her experiences, the relationship changed, and the reaction she got back was more than the Israeli-Palestine wars.

There is a lot to learn there. Sarah could have done better by processing her emotions appropriately. Abraham should not have absolved himself of every responsibility. Everyone could have done better in this situation.

Relationships evolve and have their issues, and when they do, we have to be open about the issues so that we don't go into a toxic place. Unfortunately, many God-ordained relationships have ended prematurely over time because the parties involved could not handle the evolution of such relationships.

Human beings are very dynamic, hence the need to understand how to manage that dynamism. Every man is a combination of spirit, soul, and body. This means spiritual, mental, emotional, and physical dynamics are involved in every relationship. We all switch between these components constantly in our interactions with other people. We are all at different levels of spiritual, mental, emotional, and physical development per time and all of these impact our relationships positively or negatively depending on handling.

Sometimes, people enter into a relationship on a level of understanding that is almost at par. The people involved know what is expected of each other and the roles individuals have to play in the relationship. The parties involved are at a level of understanding that is clear and acceptable. Using our case studies (Abraham, Sarah, and Hagar) as an example, it was clear that Hagar was a slave to Abraham and his wife, Sarah. It was a vertical kind of relationship where Abraham and Sarah were high up there on the relationship ladder while Hagar was at a lower level. Hence, this determined the primary dynamics of the relationship. The roles were evident, as well as the expectations.

However, things took a new turn when there was a shift in the relationship dynamics the moment Hagar, without prior notice or proper communication, was brought up to the same level as Abraham and Sarah in the relationship ladder. Apparently, Abraham and Sarah didn't realise that it was what they were doing when they danced to the tune of Sarah's idea of making Hagar a surrogate in wife matters. In their minds, they assumed that it was still the same slave-girl they acquired some years before. As such, they still expected the same level of compliance from Hagar, which was practically impossible.

Becoming a sexual partner to Abraham brought Hagar to a higher level in the relationship, at least emotionally. She had been introduced to a higher level of emotional commitment to and connection with her master, Abraham. That was a relationship evolution that was not properly managed. The dynamics had changed even though the actors were not conscious of it. It may have appeared that the dynamic was still the same, but it was not the truth.

When roles are switched in a relationship, expectations and demands will naturally shift even when not explicitly communicated. Hagar, who was now more emotionally and psychologically invested in the relationship with her master (especially), must have expected that she would be treated with more dignity since she was now acting like a wife and not just a slave. She had stepped up subconsciously, and it invariably affected how she directly related with her boss, Sarah. It was now like Hagar was saying, *'Hey, boss, we are now on the same level since I am now a bedmate with your husband and will soon be a mother of his child'* She didn't need to say it in plain terms, she just needed to act it out. And like they say, *'Action speaks louder than voice.'*

On the other hand, Abraham and (especially) Sarah were still seeing Hagar as the slave that she was. Nothing changed about her in their minds, but they were deceiving themselves. You can't give people intimate roles and not be willing to accord them the respect that the role deserves. Likewise, you can't give someone the status of a wife or mother-to-be and not be ready to satisfy the other conditions that come with that status change, especially in the way you relate with them and the expectations you now have of them.

This basic understanding will help us manage the relationships in our lives better, whether as partners, spouses, mentors, mentees, friends, family, etc. People change as they get more exposed, face challenges, change roles, change association, change location, etc. This means that expectations and demands will naturally change, too, and it is essential to manage the effects of these changes. Let's highlight a few things that help to manage relationship evolution better:

a) **Understanding:** Understanding is very critical in relationships. *'A house is built by* *wisdom and becomes strong through good sense.* (Proverbs 24:3 NLT). The establishment of any relationship is dependent on the understanding exhibited by the individuals involved. Understanding here refers to the ability to be reasonable in discerning the other person's state, desire, or need in the relationship. This helps to appreciate people's growth or changes better in a relationship and the corresponding demands or requirements. This determines if a relationship will stand the test of change.

b) **Knowledge:** *'Through knowledge, its rooms are filled with all sorts of precious riches and valuables'.* (Proverbs 24:4 NLT). Knowledge is a filler and beautifier of relationships. How beautiful and attractive a relationship will be is determined by the knowledge base of the people involved. Their knowledge of people management (thought patterns, temperaments, idiosyncrasies, hobbies, strengths, weaknesses, etc.), conflict resolution, communication, etc., ultimately determines how beautiful the relationship will be.

c) **Communication:** This is unarguably the lifeline of any relationship. 'Can two people together without agreeing on the direction'? (Amos 3:3 NLT). The agreement needed to cultivate and sustain a relationship can only be achieved through communication. Without effective communication, the evolution that is always a constant in every relationship will always lead to calamity or end in toxicity. Communication is important for explaining, clarifying, or managing the changes resulting from growth, role switches, etc., in a relationship. Things would have turned out differently between Abraham, Sarah, and Hagar if proper communication was employed. Let's paint a scenario. What if Abraham and his wife approached Hagar respectfully after Sarah came up with the idea that they could have a baby through Hagar? Imagine that Sarah (in her husband's company) approached Hagar and said something like this,

> *'Hello, Hagar, We appreciate all you have been and done for us as a servant in this house so far. We have a little request to make. God*

promised to give us a child, but from all indications, it doesn't look like that would happen anytime soon. We were wondering if you could help us facilitate this process by agreeing to sleep with my husband, get pregnant, and your child will become ours. We won't mind if the pregnancy process affects some of your responsibilities in the house. We promise to give you all the support needed if you agree to do this for us'.

This communicates value and respect for Hagar and could have helped her see things differently and act differently. Many relationships become toxic because there are unspoken expectations and unclarified assumptions. Parties in a relationship must learn to communicate without ambiguity. As the relationship evolves, it becomes more imperative to communicate. This means that the parties in a relationship must continually sharpen their communication skills. Expressing one's thoughts and desires clearly to the other person is not always as easy as it seems. It requires some tactfulness.

d) Emotional Intelligence: Humans are emotional beings. This means our emotions come to bear in our interactions. You can't separate a man from his emotions. People act based on their emotions many times. Emotions include a variety of feelings such as anger, anxiety, sadness, happiness, gratitude, disappointment, enthusiasm, frustration, satisfaction, optimism, pessimism, etc. Different experiences trigger different emotions. Emotional intelligence refers to the ability of people to identify and manage their feelings and, by extension, that of others as well. What this implies is that people are at different levels of emotional intelligence. More emotionally intelligent people will naturally relate better with others because they are aware of their own emotions and empathetic towards other people's emotions.

Emotional intelligence ensures that people take responsibility for their feelings and are sensitive to other people's feelings.

Contemplation

1. Was there any time you had to do something you wouldn't have done ordinarily? What was responsible for this?

2. Are you struggling to yield to God about anything in your life?

3. Is there any decision you made in the past that you are blaming someone else for the consequence today?

4. What do you need to do to make better decisions in life henceforth?

5. Are you in any relationship whose evolution you have not handled well? What can you do differently from now on?

HAGAR AND ISHMAEL

The Relationship between Hagar and Ishmael

Ishmael was the first biological son of Abraham. Ishmael was the son Hagar bore for Abraham. Ishmael was the stepbrother of Isaac. His mother was given to Abraham to bear children for him. Ishmael was first mentioned in scriptures in the book of Genesis when Hagar first fled from the presence of her mistress, Sarah, as a result of maltreatment from her.

> 'And the angel also said, "You are now pregnant and will give birth to a son. You are to name him Ishmael (which means 'God hears'), for the LORD, has heard your cry of distress. This son of yours will be a wild man,

as untamed as a wild donkey! He will raise his fist against everyone, and everyone will be against him. Yes, he will live in open hostility against all his relatives. Genesis 16:11-12 (NLT)

The name Ishmael is from the Hebrew word *'Yishmael'* meaning *'God will hear'* or *'God listens'*. The name *'Ishmael'* came as an answer to Hagar's cry and affliction.

Ishmael represents the reassurance that God gives every Hagar who is going through any form of affliction. Ishmael was the answer to the pain and hurt of Hagar.

God named the child Ishmael to remind her that He has seen and heard her pain and affliction.

The root word *'affliction'* used in Genesis 16:11 in the Hebrew text means *'depression'*, *'to look down on'* and *'to reduce to nothing'*. In other words, Hagar was feeling low, empty, and like nothing. God told her to call her son Ishmael which means 'God has heard your affliction'.

Not just affliction in the sense of physical pain, but the feeling that you are low and empty. The story of Hagar is the heart cry of a wounded woman. This was a woman that was wounded and sent away. In her agony, she cried out to God, and He heard her cry.

For those *'Hagars'* out there who are being abused and reduced, God has heard your cry. Your *'Ishmael'* might not be a son, but your Ishmael is the reassurance that God has given to you. Anytime Hagar saw Ishmael, she said to herself, *'God's got me'*. Your *'Ishmael'* is that thing that reminds you that God hears you when you cry out to Him.

Your own Ishmael may not be a child; it may be a job, a pastor, or a friend that, anytime you see, reminds you that God hears you, and even if you have messed up like Hagar, God still hears you.

The Mental State of Hagar Concerning Ishmael's Birth

Hagar was mentally and physically traumatised. She wasn't ready to have a child at such a young age. She also involuntarily had a sexual relationship with her mistress' husband, which she was unprepared for. Sleeping with her mistress' husband without any marriage arrangement was new to her, and she was put in an uncomfortable position with an uncertain future. Abraham and Sarah never saw Hagar as a whole person – never calling her by her name, which affected her mental health as an individual. To be seen as a mere object to be used as a surrogate for Sarah gave her a sense of low self-worth.

Being unable to make decisions for herself affected her mental health as well. That is obvious in the fact that Abraham tells Sarah that Hagar is in her hand and that she could do with her whatever she pleases. In Genesis 21, we see how Sarah continues this abuse when she tells Abraham to banish Hagar and her son to a life in the wilderness, which could have led to the demise of mother and child.

The Purpose of Ishmael

'Then God said to Abraham, "Regarding Sarai, your wife—her name will no longer be Sarai. From now on her name will be Sarah. And I will bless her and give you a son from her! Yes, I will bless her richly, and she will become the mother of many nations. Kings of nations will be among her descendants." Then Abraham bowed down to the ground, but he laughed to himself in disbelief. "How could I become a father at the age of 100?" he thought. "And how can Sarah have a baby when she is ninety years old?" So Abraham said to God, "May Ishmael live under your special blessing!" But God replied, "No—Sarah, your wife, will give birth to a son for you. You will name him Isaac and I will confirm my covenant with him and his descendants as an everlasting covenant. As for Ishmael, I will bless him also, just as you have asked. I will make him extremely fruitful and multiply his descendants. He will become the father of twelve princes, and I will make him a great nation'. Genesis 17:15-20 (NLT)

Ishmael was not the promised child and could have died or probably not been a part of the story, but his story was captured in black and white in the scriptures because God had a plan for his life. God eventually gave him a promise of his own. There is no child that God doesn't have a plan for. God has a plan for even our own mistakes. Even if you make a mistake, God can redesign your mistake for His glory.

Looking at the story in retrospect, God gave Abraham a word, and they didn't leave it alone to bear fruit, so they tried to act out of impatience. It is evident that Abraham and Sarah, in a bid to help God, made a mistake that resulted in Ishmael. Despite the circumstances surrounding the birth of Ishmael and him not being the promised child, God still made a great nation of him.

As God's people, we might make mistakes as humans, but God still weaves our mistakes into a grand design. Some of us are living other people's mistakes, and we can't do anything about it. When people's mess affects our lives,

God has a way of using it for His purpose. In Hagar's life, over and over again, she was the victim of the mistakes of other people, and every time she wanted to give up, God was always showing up to say, *'I have got you'*. That is what God does; He turns around our mistakes and makes something good out of them.

Don't Let Go of Your Ishmael

'When Isaac grew up and was about to be weaned, Abraham prepared a huge feast to celebrate the occasion. But Sarah saw Ishmael—the son of Abraham and her Egyptian servant Hagar—making fun of her son, Isaac. So she turned to Abraham and demanded, "Get rid of that slave woman and her son. He is not going to share the inheritance with my son, Isaac. I won't have it!" This upset Abraham very much because Ishmael was his son. But God told Abraham, "Do not be upset over the boy and your servant. Do whatever Sarah tells you, for Isaac is the son through whom your descendants will be counted. But I will also

make a nation of the descendants of Hagar's son because he is your son, too." So Abraham got up early the next morning, prepared food and a container of water, and strapped them on Hagar's shoulders. Then he sent her away with their son, and she wandered aimlessly in the wilderness of Beersheba. When the water was gone, she put the boy in the shade of a bush. Then she went and sat down by herself about a hundred yards away. "I don't want to watch the boy die," she said as she burst into tears. But God heard the boy crying, and the angel of God called to Hagar from heaven, "Hagar, what's wrong? Do not be afraid! God has heard the boy crying as he lies there. Go to him and comfort him, for I will make a great nation from his descendants." Then God opened Hagar's eyes, and she saw a well full of water. She quickly filled her water container and gave the boy a drink. And God was with the boy as he grew up in the wilderness. He became a skillful archer, and he settled in the wilderness of Paran. His mother arranged for him to marry a woman from the land of Egypt'. Genesis 21:8-21 (NLT)

If Ishmael had stayed, Isaac would not have been counted as the heir, so Ishmael had to leave. When Sarah said Abraham should send Hagar and Ishmael away, Abraham was upset not because of Hagar but because of Ishmael, his son. At this point, Hagar had been used and put aside. This also shows that Abraham had an emotional attachment to Ishmael because He was upset about getting rid of Ishmael until God told him to do what Sarah had said. Abraham sent Hagar and Ishmael away with only food and a container of water. He also sent them away on foot despite his wealth. That would have been a low moment for Hagar because she was sent to wander. Soon, their supplies of water and food were finished. As she wandered in perplexity, each time she looked at Ishmael, she remembered that God heard her.

A discussion between a husband and a wife got her pregnant. Also, a conversation between a husband and a wife led to her expulsion to the wilderness because Ishmael was just making fun of Isaac. Hagar didn't have a family to go back to, and she also had a child, which was extra baggage. She was lost, and her supply of water was exhausted. She put Ishmael a hundred yards away because she didn't want to watch him die. Finally, Hagar gave up on Ishmael.

Hagar didn't want to hear the boy crying, but God heard the boy crying. This time, God responded not to the cry of Hagar but the cry of Ishmael. Then the angel of the Lord told her to lift her child because God had heard his cry. This wasn't the time to give up. Until she lifted her child, she did not see the well. God told her to pick up her dream, and He will show her the way.

When you pick up your dream, God shows you the way. When God looks at your *'Ishmael'*, He doesn't see a dying child or a vision; God sees a nation. Most times when things are not working as planned with our vision, we abandon our dream when our dreams are actually calling out to us. Even when you have run out of resources, don't let your dream die. When you lift your dream, God will show up for you.

No matter how far you wander away, God will find a way to bring you back. No matter what you do, God is always on your side. God understands our humanity, and He has made His accommodations for us to be human beings. He knows we will mess up, but He has made a way for us.

Therefore, you don't need to let go of your Ishmael. It could be a child you gave birth to out of wedlock or even the product of a rape. That doesn't mean they cannot be a blessing to you and others. Ishmael may remind you of your pain, but he should also remind you, much more, of the faithfulness of God; the fact that God is still with you even in your mess.

Contemplation

1. What is your 'Ishmael' presently?

2. What mistake have you made in the past that you have seen God turn around for your good?

3. What vision have you abandoned that you need to pick up again?

4. Are you in any situation at the moment where you are about to give up on something very promising?

Chapter 5

HAGAR AND GOD

How do we know about God as children? Who would have introduced Hagar to her God? At the time when Hagar was born, the Egyptians were worshipping several gods. So while Hagar was growing up, there is a probability that she must have been introduced to one of the gods of Egypt by her parents, and that would have been the god she knew.

How do we see God as children? What is the image of God that our parents have painted to us as children? As a child, Hagar must have had an idea of God as a supreme being. As children, our parents paint a picture of God as a superhero to us – someone that you pray to and can help you when you are in trouble. So, Hagar must have had this same picture of whatever god was presented to her.

When Hagar was handed over as a slave, she must have felt really bad to think that her god had allowed her to be sold into slavery. After she was handed over as a slave, the turn of events would have given her a feeling of utter disappointment of her image of a god; since her god, who is supposed to be some form of a superhero to protect her in times of trouble, couldn't stop her from being sold into slavery. Hagar was probably worshipping one of the idols of Egypt before she became Abram's slave. Her first encounter with the true Living God was in Abram's household.

Hagar must have left Egypt in a deplorable state that her parents could not save her and her so-called gods couldn't save her either. In the journey from Egypt to Canaan, she must have been praying all through the way, waiting hopefully for her gods to save her, and there was still no response or any encounter. That was probably the reason why she called the Living God *'The God who hears me'*. Her journey from Egypt to Canaan was the birth of her encounter with God. She needed someone to answer the questions of her heart, and there was none.

Hagar's First Encounter with God

Hagar only found her identity when she met with God. **In the Bible, Abraham and Sarah never called her by name. The first person that called her by name was the angel of God.**

> *'The angel of the LORD found Hagar beside a spring of water in the wilderness, along the road to Shur. The angel said to her,* **"Hagar, Sarai's servant,** *where have you come from, and where are you going?" "I'm running away from my mistress, Sarai," she replied'.*
> Genesis 16:7-8 NLT (Emphasis added)

This happened when Hagar initially fled from her mistress. She had become pregnant and began to despise Sarah. When you strip away her being a slave girl, she was an actual person who was pregnant. She did not plan to get pregnant by a man that she was serving. Hagar was interrupted by God. God saw a rudderless ship moving in the ocean without direction. God saw a young lady that was traumatised, with no identity, and whose bosses had never called by name. God interrupted her life.

When you experience a divine interruption, God calls you by who you truly are. When we are divinely interrupted, God strips the labels that others have put on us, and God calls us by our true identity. For example, when Hagar ran away, God identified her and asked her, *'Where have you come from and where are you going'?* She answered, *'I am running away from my mistress, Sarai'*. She told God where she was coming from, but she didn't tell God where she was going. Her past had always defined her life, and she had no vision of the future. She had nothing to run towards; she was just moving aimlessly. She thought that running away was the answer, but God was about to redirect her life. She didn't know that she had to go back there. She thought by running from the problem; she would find a solution.

We can't answer every question. We don't know all that happened, but what we do know is that this was a young, vulnerable, broken pregnant woman. She had no identity, but God saw her and interrupted her life. She didn't pray, yet God showed up.

You may be *'Hagar'* reading this book right now. You may be on the run, not knowing where exactly you are heading towards. The good news is that God is calling you by your name and saying, *'Stop running'!* He knows you. You have an identity. Hagar was jobless, homeless, without a husband, pregnant, and running aimlessly in the wilderness. She didn't even know where she was going, and her life was divinely interrupted. Hagar was in the lowest of the lows of her life, but God called her by name and gave her a true identity. Hagar knew what she was running away from. She was running away from her pain. She was running away from her lack of identity, but the angel of the Lord said she should return. Most likely, Hagar was probably running to a place where she could call home.

We always think about God as someone that should save us in our times of trouble, but in Hagar's case, she encounters God, and the first thing He tells her is to go back to her oppression. That was a contrast to the image of God she had in her head. God told Hagar to go back and submit to her mistress. Sometimes, God would take us back to a particular place because our sojourn there is not yet complete. With God, we won't always understand the **'WHY'**, why something happens, or why we go through a trial. With God, you can't always get an answer.

> *'The angel of the LORD said to her, "Return to your mistress, and submit to her authority."'*. Genesis 16:9 (NLT)

Much of our image of Christianity is comfort and luxury, but Christianity is actually greater than our personal convenience. Sometimes, Christianity involves you going through challenges that are not convenient because there is a bigger picture of God's purpose. If you see life as bigger than your personal comfort, your perspective about problems will change. You will see problems in a totally different light.

Hagar's breakthrough was in her offspring, and God did not want Ishmael to be raised fatherless. Ishmael had to be part of the blessing of Abraham. So God said, *'Yes, you may run, but this is not the time to leave'.*

When God keeps us longer at a junction, it is beyond what our human understanding can put together. Many times, our reaction would be to run away from the situation. But, God would not take her back to being messed up.

> *'Then he added, "I will give you more descendants than you can count" And the angel also said, "You are now pregnant and will give birth to a son. You are to name him Ishmael (which means 'God hears'), for the Lord, has heard your cry of distress'.* Genesis 16:10-11 (NLT)

She got the name of her child in her first encounter. Sarah and Abraham didn't name the child; it was God who named him. So Hagar was the first woman in the Bible that God made a covenant with, and she was the first person in the scriptures that God declared pregnant and gave a prophecy about her child.

The instruction to return was a painful decision that came with fear and trepidation, but it was the key. If she had walked away, Ishmael would have been a *nobody*. If she had run away with the child in her womb, Ishmael would not have been circumcised, and circumcision was part of God's covenant with Abraham to bless him. Ishmael would not have been nurtured in the right space. There are a lot of people who have left their *Abrahams* too early. A lot of people have left their God-given spiritual covering too early.

This book is not prescribing that you stay in an abusive and unhealthy relationship. What we are saying is that you find God in your situation. No one would have told Hagar to go back to Abraham's house except God. When you have an encounter with God, and He tells you to do anything, you should obey it. What doesn't make sense to us might be what God wants.

What makes a decision right is the presence of God. Even if she left eventually, as long as God didn't go with her, it would have been a wrong decision. God's presence is what makes our decisions in life right.

Hagar's Second Encounter with God

'But Sarah saw Ishmael—the son of Abraham and her Egyptian servant Hagar—making fun of her son, Isaac. So she turned to Abraham and demanded, "Get rid of that slave woman and her son. He is not going to share the inheritance with my son, Isaac. I won't have it!" This upset Abraham very much because Ishmael was his son. But God told Abraham, "Do not be upset over the boy and your servant. Do whatever Sarah tells you, for Isaac is the son through whom your descendants will be counted. But I will also make a nation of the descendants of Hagar's son because he is your son, too." So Abraham got up early the next morning, prepared food and a container of water, and strapped them on Hagar's shoulders. Then he sent her away

with their son, and she wandered aimlessly in the wilderness of Beersheba. When the water was gone, she put the boy in the shade of a bush. Then she went and sat down by herself about a hundred yards away. "I don't want to watch the boy die," she said, as she burst into tears. But God heard the boy crying, and the angel of God called to Hagar from heaven, "Hagar, what's wrong? Do not be afraid! God has heard the boy crying as he lies there. Go to him and comfort him, for I will make a great nation from his descendants." Then God opened Hagar's eyes, and she saw a well full of water. She quickly filled her water container and gave the boy a drink. And God was with the boy as he grew up in the wilderness. He became a skillful archer, and he settled in the wilderness of Paran. His mother arranged for him to marry a woman from the land of Egypt'. Genesis 21:9-21(NLT)

At this point in her life, Hagar had forgotten about her first encounter with God. Hagar had forgotten that the word Ishmael means *'God had heard me'*. Until you pick up your *'Ishmael'*, you will not see the way. When God called her this time, He didn't address her as Hagar slave of Sarah; He just called her Hagar, which is very profound. This time around, it was obvious that her phase with Abraham and Sarah was now over. That part of her story was complete. They were no longer her reference point, and she wasn't going back this time.

Hagar was so perplexed that she had forgotten that the child she had given up to die was known by God and named by God. Ishmael was no longer her mistake but a symbol of God's intervention. Ishmael was now God's project. In fact, God called out Hagar this time because He heard Ishmael's voice,

> 'But God heard the boy crying, and the angel of God called to Hagar from heaven, "Hagar, what's wrong? Do not be afraid! God has heard the boy crying as he lies there. Go to him and comfort him, for I will make a great nation from his descendants"'. Genesis 21:17-18 (NLT).

Isn't that interesting? God stepped into the situation this time because of Ishmael. God heard his cry and showed up. Though Hagar had gotten to a point where she was willing to let go of her pain and mistake, God said no because there was still a plan for Ishmael. Ishmael was going to become a great nation. Ishmael was still going to enjoy the fatherhood of God as well as Hagar. It may be easy for an earthly father to forsake or disown their children because of their mistakes, but God is never like that. God is ever willing to embrace us and love us even with our mistakes.

God's love is unconditional. He is always thinking of how to restore us, not to destroy us. He is ever ready to turn our mistakes around for good. He will turn our pain points into reasons to rejoice. In God, our *Ishmaels* are still covered. His fatherhood remains a constant and can always be trusted. Glory to God!

Contemplation

1. What image of God was painted to you by your parents or guardians when you were young?

2. How do you see God for yourself presently?

3. Are you running aimlessly at the moment? Do you know where exactly you are going in life?

4. Is there something God has asked you to do that feels very difficult for you to even think of doing?

Chapter 6

HAGAR AND YOU

At this point in the book, you may still be wondering how *Hagar* relates to you as the reader. A lot of us would not be under the covers of the sheets of Abraham in the cold of the night or whenever he wants it without our permission. Not many of us would want to be pregnant under the heavy-handedness of Sarah.

How many of us live our lives as a result of other people's decisions and have been suffering the consequences? How many of us have been robbed of our childhood? How many of us have given up our dreams and Ishmaels?

If any of these (above) sounds like you, then you should already understand how the story of

Hagar relates to you. So, as we come to the end of this book, let's take a last look at how Hagar relates to you today.

A Faulty Background

Looking at Hagar's background, how she was taken away from her family at an early age, and bringing it to the context of our world today, she must have suffered from anxiety, isolation and depression, and she must have been suicidal due to her being separated from what she was used to. A young girl today who is in Hagar's shoes would most likely not cope with her situation.

There are several instances of young girls that have been sexually abused by their masters who got so broken that it led them into insanity or severe mental health issues and other related traumas. In the Bible, there isn't any reference to show that Hagar struggled with her new reality. Instead, it shows how things have changed between the time of Hagar and the present day. Hagar adapted to what happened to her because she didn't have a choice, but today, there is a choice not to adapt because there are more opportunities to get help and support.

The story could have been very different if it was in our modern-day. Unfortunately, Hagar didn't have the luxury of choices like today. Today, Hagar could have aborted the child out of anger because she fought with Sarah, her mistress, who chased her out of the house. In our generation, abortion out of retaliation is something that could have happened, or she could have given up the child to another family.

We don't know why Hagar was handed over as a slave, but it is most likely because she was born to a family that didn't have much privileges and influence in society. In our world today, if your parents are struggling and they can't do very much for you, it is most likely for them to hand you over to a relative who can do better and give you better opportunities such as education. If Hagar's parents were influential in society, they would never hand over their daughter to Sarah, regardless of whoever she was.

Whatever the reason for Hagar being given away as a slave by her parents, Hagar was part of a transaction, and it was an unfair transaction. That tells us that life could really be unfair. There are a lot of us whose lives are transactional even at this age. We live our lives based on the transactions that other people make. So, we have a beautiful, talented, and blessed woman who found herself in an unfortunate place. No one can say that being a slave is comfortable. She did not just become a slave; she literally became Abraham's property. She lost her sense of self and identity.

You may be reading this book now, and you don't even have ownership over your life. You might have a source of income, yet your life is a result of the transactions of other people, and that is a recurring pattern we see in the life of Hagar. Hagar became Abraham's slave in Egypt, but she ended up in Canaan. Likewise, some of us have jobs that we think are leading us somewhere, and they end up leading us nowhere or into places that we shouldn't be. Many people do things not voluntarily but under the pressure of other people, and the consequences are far-reaching.

This book is for you if you find yourself in a messy situation and do not understand how you got there. This book is for you if you find yourself in a broken relationship with your source or network. This book is for you if you find yourself isolated in a place far away from home. This is so because Hagar's story reflects your personal story.

Unplanned for

In the story, it is not clearly stated whether or not Hagar's consent was sought about the decision to bear a child for Abraham. Hagar was a full-grown woman who had full volition whether to spread her legs or close them, yet she was asked to mother a child. As a slave, she had no option. She was put in a challenging situation, and it seemed like she had no choice but to agree.

There are many times in life when we are vulnerable. We tend to make decisions to satisfy other people and make them happy. How many girls have abandoned their homes and parents to elope with a lover? Many people find themselves in the kind of situation where people have taken advantage of them. None of these was about Hagar's plans.

For you reading this book, our advice is that whenever you are in that place of vulnerability and are overwhelmed by your emotions about making a decision that you really don't want to, it is advisable to talk to someone more experienced to avoid regrets. Don't make a decision based on your feelings.

Hagar, after she volunteered to be a mum for a couple finding it difficult to have their child, was treated very harshly and sent out of the house on one occasion by her mistress, Sarah. So maybe you are a young woman out there, and you are pregnant even though you never planned it, and it's like a burden that frustrates you, and as a result, people no longer treat you nicely. Maybe you are an ex-convict who has made a couple of wrong choices, and everything is against you.

In almost every single situation, you will find yourself wanting to run away from your pain. That was what Hagar felt. Hagar woke up, every single day of that pregnancy, not just in physical pain but also the emotional pain of being maltreated by a woman she helped. Maybe you have a horrible boss who doesn't treat you with respect and thinks they have power over you because of the contract that you have signed. Yet, you still have to show up because you don't have a better choice. That is Hagar in you.

Mislabelled

Abraham and Sarah never called Hagar by her name. All through the Bible, she was always referred to as property. You might also be going through a similar situation like Hagar, where people never see any good in you and always refer to you by your race or background, which could be very dehumanising. In society today, people label other people by their physical appearances, such as skin colour, race, origin, etc., and they lose their sense of identity because of that.

This is very common among African women, whose identity is defined by their kids or husbands. It's either you are the mother of someone or the wife of someone. They lose their sense of individuality because people define their identity by other people. You will never find your true identity when your life is determined based on who or what is around you. If your kids define your life, what exactly would happen, and what would your life be like when they are all grown up and eventually leave home?

Maybe you are finding it hard to get back into society because you have spent some time in jail, and people just seem to label you by your past and give you no chance to prove that you are not that person anymore.

Divine Encounter

The *'Ishmael'* in your life doesn't have to be a child, it might be a dream or a vision that you are holding on to or a business idea that you have always had, but you abandoned because you don't know how to handle all the pressure that it entails.

Hagar got the guidance of the angel, which is what a lot of us are craving. For instance, you may have a business idea for which you need a mentor or a coach in that area who is more knowledgeable to guide you on the road to accomplishing your goal.

A lot of people are in the world living in fear of an uncertain future, not knowing where they are going or what they should be doing. That was precisely what happened to Ishmael and Hagar. Hagar and Ishmael were sent out of Abraham's house, and on the way, their bread and water got exhausted.

Hagar wanted a promising future for Ishmael, and right then, he was about to die of thirst. You might find yourself in such a situation like Hagar. Always seek help and never suffer in secret. Don't carry your burden alone. Always share because you never know where your help is going to come from.

The most crucial experience in Hagar's life is not the fact that she was sold into slavery or that she was used and abused by Abraham and Sarah, or that she was unloved and unwanted.

Instead, the most defining moment in Hagar's life is that she had a divine encounter with God.

That is all this book is about. It is about introducing you to Jesus. It is about introducing you to the power of God and how He can transform your life.

There Is Still Hope for You

No matter what happens, your life doesn't have to be defined by the name people call you, your experiences, or that they don't call you by your name. What matters is that there is something God has given to you; you carry something of value. God wants you to see yourself the way He sees you. He has heard your tears and agony about how bad you have been treated, and He sent an angel. This book is your angel. This book is meant to give you hope, comfort, and strength. No matter what has happened, no matter what you look like, there is still hope.

> *'Even a tree has more hope! If it is cut down, it will sprout again like a new seedling'.* Job 14:7 (NLT)

There is hope for you; it doesn't matter how hopeless things may seem. This book is your angel; this book is God's interruption of your life. This book is God showing forth His mercy and taking ownership of your life again. This book is a reminder of what God can do through you.

This book is a wake-up call to you to stop judging yourself and quit having that sense of poor self-worth or low self-esteem. God is calling you by your name today and saying that He cares for you. He has seen your pain and your tears in silence, and He has heard the palpitations of your heart. He has seen the lonely, cold and weary journey, and this book is a divine response to your cry of being unloved and unwanted. So lift your head from the dust and look around, for there is a provision of water right where you are. If you have not met Jesus, now is the time to do so. All you have to do is say this prayer:

> *Lord Jesus, I know I don't have a relationship with you but I want you. I humbly accept you as my Lord and Saviour and I ask that you come into my life in Jesus' name.*

Contemplation

1. Having read thus far, in what way are you Hagar presently? How does her story relate to you?

2. In what way have you lost hope in yourself? What do you need to do to believe again?

3. What are your main learning points from this book, and what steps will you be taking to make them count in your life?

Meet The Authors

Niyi Borire - Paul Onukaogu - Senayon Amosu - Herve Kadiya - Omor Bello - Ruth Ejiwale - Tofunmi Ejiwale

NIYI BORIRE

Niyi Borire is an award-winning neurologist, Amazon best-selling author, lecturer, author, and change agent.

He has written three books, including his autobiography titled Navigating Change: Timeless Secrets for Growth in an Ever-Changing World.

Niyi is on a mission to help people navigate change without losing their purpose, identity, and individuality.

He is the Director of Southwest Neurology and a neuroscience lecturer at the University of New South Wales.

Niyi is also the founder and director of Changemakers Book Club

PAUL ONUKAOGU

Paul Onukaogu is a deep thinking and well-spoken individual with a vibrant and welcoming personality. He is an environmental engineer who is passionate about his work whilst passionate about making positive impacts and significance in his field.

Paul is also the founder of B2M (Boy-To-Man), a not-for-profit organisation with a vision to become a platform that will nurture and groom boys into becoming the men that they are destined to be

Paul currently leads the youth and young adults in his church, but above all, he is a loving husband to his wife Annie and a father to his daughter Daniella.

SENAYON AMOSU

Senayon Amosu is a vibrant, intelligent, and enthusiastic individual. She is a primary school teacher, helping children be the best they can possibly be and reach for the stars. She extends her love for learning and teaching the future generation with her tutoring business 'Shays Tutoring Class' for Primary students.

Senayon is passionate about helping others who are in need. In 2017 she took a trip to Cambodia to build houses for the less fortunate and visit orphanages.

Senayon is also a poet who writes many spoken words on various issues around the world and uses her platform to share the gospel. She is a daughter to Viavo and Aramide Amosu.

HERVE KADIYA

Herve Kadiya, better known by his stage name "Herve HK", is a gospel, motivational hip hop artist born in the Democratic Republic of Congo. He's also a full-time service technician and full-time student, pursuing his Bachelor of Business in Organisational Technology Management.

Herve HK has released two major projects: an Ep' Unashamed' and an album 'All for you'. These two projects are a representation of his love for God. He is currently working on his third project, which will be released towards the end of 2021.

Herve HK believes that his songs will help empower generations, especially the younger generations, to be unashamed (Romans 1:16) about the gospel here in Australia, New Zealand, and all over the world. He also believes in helping this generation express their God-given talent and gifts freely and unashamedly.

OMOH BELLO

Omoh Bello is a talented Nigerian and creative storyteller. She believes that everybody has a story, and there is something to learn and be inspired by from every experience.

A graduate of Future Journalism and Creative Media, Omoh has independently produced short documentaries and was part of a team that produced a short film.

Omoh's belief in the power of storytelling led her to create a platform and produce 'The Backstory', an online series where everyday people share their stories and others can draw strength.

Omoh is also an imminent portrait photographer and Fashion designer.

RUTH EJIWALE

Dunni Ejiwale is an experienced community educator with a demonstrated history of working in non-profit organisations. She believes that everyone has a calling/purpose in life and was driven to co-publish this book because of her passion for helping people and her keen interest to make an impact.

Dunni is a powerful force in the workplace, where she uses her positive attitude and tireless energy to encourage others to work hard and succeed. In addition, she is inspired daily by her family and friends.

TOFUNMI EJIWALE

Tofunmi Ejiwale is an ambitious and innovative research scientist who is passionate about people and wants to use her scientific knowledge to improve everyday human lives. She is also a writer and lover of God.

Tofunmi is keenly passionate about personal growth by pushing herself beyond her comfort zone, engaging in activities that stretch her and building her emotional strength. In the words of Les Brown, her ultimate desire is to 'live fully and die empty."

www.ingramcontent.com/pod-product-compliance
Lightning Source LLC
Chambersburg PA
CBHW031254290426
44109CB00012B/576